Contents

I0415542

EnergySavers

Right in your own home, you have the power to save money and energy. Saving energy reduces our nation's overall demand for resources needed to make energy, and increasing your energy efficiency is like adding another clean energy source to our electric power grid.

This guide shows you how easy it is to cut your energy use at home and also on the road. The easy, practical solutions for saving energy include tips you can use today—from the roof and landscaping to appliances and lights. They are good for your wallet and for the environment—and actions that you take help reduce our national needs to produce or import more energy, thereby improving our energy security.

Tips for Renters and Property Owners

If you rent, or if you own a rental unit, you can use many of the tips throughout this guide to save money and energy!

Renters
You can reduce your utility bills by following the tips in the Lighting, Heating and Cooling (if you control the thermostat), Appliances, Home Office and Home Electronics, Windows, and Transportation sections. Encourage your landlord to follow these tips as well. They'll save energy and money, improving your comfort and lowering your utility bills even more.

Property Owners
Nearly all of the information in this guide applies to rental units. The chapter on Your Home's Energy Use focuses on air leaks, insulation, heating and cooling, roofing, landscaping, water heating, windows, appliances, and renewable energy.

Find even more information about saving money and energy at home by visiting energysavers.gov.

To learn more about U.S. Department of Energy (DOE) programs in energy efficiency and renewable energy, visit the Office of Energy Efficiency and Renewable Energy website at eere.energy.gov.

Save Money and Energy Today

An energy-efficient home will keep your family comfortable while saving you money. Whether you take simple steps or make larger investments to make your home more efficient, you'll see lower energy bills. Over time, those savings will typically pay for the cost of improvements and put money back in your pocket. Your home may also be more attractive to buyers when you sell.

The 113 million residences in America today collectively use an estimated 22% of the country's energy. Unfortunately, a lot of energy is wasted through leaky windows or ducts, old appliances, or inefficient heating and cooling systems. When we waste energy in our homes, we are throwing away money that could be used for other things. The typical U.S. family spends at least $2,000 a year on home utility bills. You can lower this amount by up to 25% through following the Long Term Savings Tips in this guide.

The key to these savings is to take a whole-house approach—by viewing your home as an energy system with interdependent parts. For example, your heating system is not just a furnace—it's a heat-delivery system that starts at the furnace and delivers heat throughout your home using a network of ducts. Even a top-of-the-line, energy-efficient furnace will waste a lot of fuel if the ducts, walls, attic, windows, and doors are leaky or poorly insulated. Taking a whole-house approach to saving energy ensures that dollars you invest to save energy are spent wisely.

Tips to Save Energy Today
Easy low-cost and no-cost ways to save energy.

- Install a programmable thermostat to lower utility bills and manage your heating and cooling systems efficiently.

- Air dry dishes instead of using your dishwasher's drying cycle.

- Turn things off when you are not in the room such as lights, TVs, entertainment systems, and your computer and monitor.

- Plug home electronics, such as TVs and DVD players, into power strips; turn the power strips off when the equipment is not in use—TVs and DVDs in standby mode still use several watts of power.

- Lower the thermostat on your water heater to 120°F.

- Take short showers instead of baths and use low-flow showerheads for additional energy savings.

- Wash only full loads of dishes and clothes.

- Air dry clothes.

- Check to see that windows and doors are closed when heating or cooling your home.

- Drive sensibly; aggressive driving such as speeding, and rapid acceleration and braking, wastes fuel.

- Look for the ENERGY STAR® label on light bulbs, home appliances, electronics, and other products. ENERGY STAR products meet strict efficiency guidelines set by the U.S. Environmental Protection Agency and the U.S. Department of Energy.

- Visit energysavers.gov for more energy-saving ideas.

A home energy assessment (sometimes referred to as an energy audit) will show what parts of your house use the most energy and suggest the best ways to cut energy costs. You can conduct a simple home energy assessment by doing it yourself (DIY) or, for a more detailed assessment, contact your local utility or an energy auditor. Also, you can learn more about home energy audits and find free tools and calculators on energysavers.gov, the Residential Services Network at resnet.us, or the Building Performance Institute at bpi.org.

DIY Energy Assessment Tips

- Check the insulation in your attic, exterior and basement walls, ceilings, floors, and crawl spaces.

To determine the insulation R-values in different parts of your home, visit the Air Leaks and Insulation section of energysavers.gov.

- Check for air leaks around your walls, ceilings, windows, doors, light and plumbing fixtures, switches, and electrical outlets.
- Check for open fireplace dampers.
- Make sure your appliances and heating and cooling systems are properly maintained. Check your owner's manuals for the recommended maintenance.
- Study your family's lighting needs and look for ways to use controls— like sensors, dimmers, or timers— to reduce lighting use.

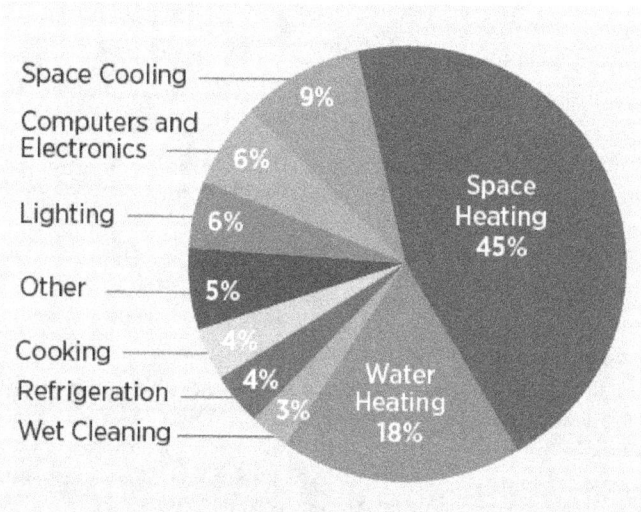

Space Cooling — 9%
Computers and Electronics — 6%
Lighting — 6%
Other — 5%
Cooking — 4%
Refrigeration — 4%
Wet Cleaning — 3%
Space Heating 45%
Water Heating 18%

How We Use Energy in Our Homes

Heating accounts for the biggest portion of your utility bills. *Source: 2010 Buildings Energy Data Book, Table 2.1.1 Residential Primary Energy Consumption, by Year and Fuel Type.*

Cool ▮▮▮▮▮▮▮▮▮▮ Hot

Photo from Infraspection Institute, Inc.

Heat Loss from a House

A picture is worth...in this case, lost heating dollars. This thermal image—taken by a professional energy auditor—shows warm air escaping through windows and cracks. The red shows where the most warm air is escaping.

Your Whole-House Plan

After you know where your home is losing energy, make a plan by asking yourself a few questions:

- How much money do you spend on energy?
- Where are your greatest energy losses?
- How long will it take for an investment in energy efficiency to pay for itself in energy cost savings?
- Do the energy-saving measures provide additional benefits that are important to you—for example, increased comfort from installing double-paned, efficient windows?
- How long do you plan to own your current home?
- Can you do the job yourself or do you need a contractor?
- What is your budget?
- How much time do you have for maintenance and repairs?

Planning smart purchases and home improvements will maximize your energy efficiency and save you the most money.

A more advanced alternative to performing a DIY energy assessment is to get advice from your state energy office, utility, or an independent energy auditor (see References for professional organizations). A professional energy auditor uses special test equipment to find air leaks, areas lacking insulation, and malfunctioning equipment. The auditor analyzes how well your home's energy systems work together, and compares the analysis to your utility bills. After gathering information about your home, the auditor will recommend cost-effective energy improvements that enhance comfort and safety. Some will also estimate how soon your investment in efficiency upgrades will pay off.

Smart Meters and a Smarter Power Grid

Millions of smart meters have been installed across the country. Smart meters provide two-way communication between you and your utility, helping your utility know about blackouts, for example. This helps utilities to maintain more reliable electrical service.

Smart meters can be used with home energy management systems such as Web-based tools that your utility provides or devices that can be installed in your home. Smart meters can display your home energy use, help you find ways to save energy and money, and even allow you to remotely adjust your thermostat or turn appliances off.

Time-Based Electricity Rates

To help reduce their peak power demands and save money, many utilities are introducing programs that encourage their customers to use electricity during off-peak hours. The programs pass on the savings to you, the customer, through rebates or reduced electricity rates.

Smart meters and home energy management systems allow customers to program how and when their home uses energy. Such programs might charge you the actual cost of power at any one time, ranging from high prices during times of peak demand to low prices during off-peak hours. If you are able to shift your power use to off-peak times—such as running your dishwasher late in the evening—these programs can save you money while helping your utility.

Time-based rates are very attractive to owners of plug-in hybrids and electric vehicles since typically these vehicles are recharged at night. See the Transportation section for more information.

Air Leaks and Insulation

Improving your home's insulation and sealing air leaks are the fastest and most cost-effective ways to reduce energy waste and make the most of your energy dollars. Be sure to seal air leaks before you insulate, because insulating materials won't block leaks.

Sealing Air Leaks

Air leaks can waste a lot of your energy dollars. One of the quickest energy- and money-saving tasks you can do is caulk, seal, and weather strip all seams, cracks, and openings to the outside.

Tips for Sealing Air Leaks

- Test your home for air tightness. On a windy day, carefully hold a lit incense stick or a smoke pen next to your windows, doors, electrical boxes, plumbing fixtures, electrical outlets, ceiling fixtures, attic hatches, and other places where air may leak. If the smoke stream travels horizontally, you have located an air leak that may need caulking, sealing, or weatherstripping.
- Caulk and weatherstrip doors and windows that leak air.
- Caulk and seal air leaks where plumbing, ducting, or electrical wiring comes through walls, floors, ceilings, and soffits over cabinets.
- Install foam gaskets behind outlet and switch plates on walls.
- Inspect dirty spots in your insulation for air leaks and mold. Seal leaks with low-expansion spray foam made for this purpose and install house flashing if needed.
- Look for dirty spots on your ceiling paint and carpet, which may indicate air leaks at interior wall/ceiling joints and wall/floor joists, and caulk them.

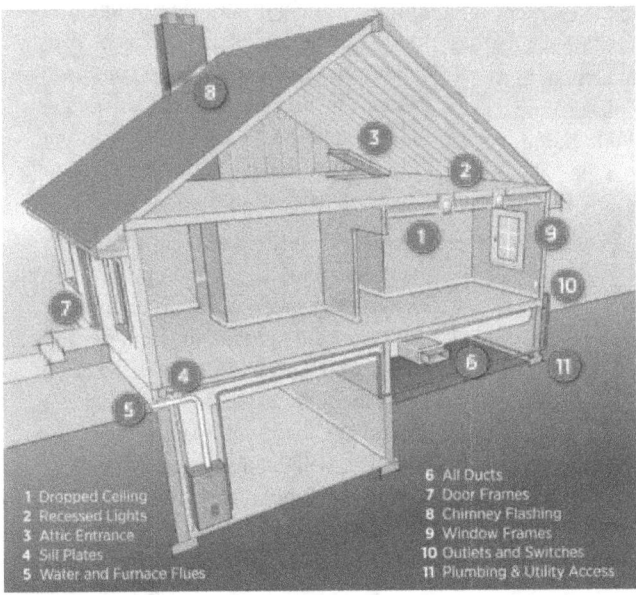

Sources of Air Leaks in Your Home

Areas that leak air into and out of your home cost you a lot of money. The areas listed in the illustration are the most common sources of air leaks.

1 Dropped Ceiling
2 Recessed Lights
3 Attic Entrance
4 Sill Plates
5 Water and Furnace Flues
6 All Ducts
7 Door Frames
8 Chimney Flashing
9 Window Frames
10 Outlets and Switches
11 Plumbing & Utility Access

- Cover single-pane windows with storm windows or replace them with more efficient double-pane low-emissivity windows. See the Windows section for more information.
- Use foam sealant on larger gaps around windows, baseboards, and other places where air may leak out.
- Cover your kitchen exhaust fan to stop air leaks when not in use.
- Check your dryer vent to be sure it is not blocked. This will save energy and may prevent a fire.
- Replace door bottoms and thresholds with ones that have pliable sealing gaskets.
- Keep the fireplace flue damper tightly closed when not in use.
- Seal air leaks around fireplace chimneys, furnaces, and gas-fired water heater vents with fire-resistant materials such as sheet metal or sheetrock and furnace cement caulk.

Fireplace flues are made from metal, and over time repeated heating and cooling can cause the metal to warp or break, creating a channel for air loss. To seal your flue when not in use, consider an inflatable chimney balloon. Inflatable chimney balloons fit beneath your fireplace flue when not in use, are made from durable plastic, and can be removed easily and reused hundreds of times. If you forget to remove the balloon before making a fire, the balloon will automatically deflate within seconds of coming into contact with heat.

Insulation

Insulation is made from a variety of materials, and it usually comes in four types: rolls and batts, loose-fill, rigid foam, and foam-in-place.

*Rolls and batts—or blankets—*are flexible products made from mineral fibers, such as fiberglass and rock wool. They are available in widths suited to standard spacing of wall studs and attic or floor joists: 2 in. x 4 in. walls can hold R-13 or R-15 batts; 2 in. x 6 in. walls can use R-19 or R-21 products.

Loose-fill insulation is usually made of fiberglass, rock wool, or cellulose in the form of loose fibers or fiber pellets. It should be blown into spaces using special pneumatic equipment. The blown-in material conforms readily to odd-sized building cavities and attics with wires, ducts, and pipes, making it well suited for places where it is difficult to effectively install other types of insulation.

Rigid foam insulation is typically more expensive than rolls and batts or loose-fill insulation, but it is very effective in exterior wall sheathing, interior sheathing for basement walls, and special applications such as attic hatches. Foam insulation R-values range from R-4 to R-6.5 per inch of thickness, which is up to 2 times greater than most other insulating materials of the same thickness.

Foam-in-place insulation can be blown into walls, on attic surfaces, or under floors to insulate and reduce air leakage. You can use the small pressurized cans of foam-in-place insulation to reduce air leakage in holes and cracks such as window and door frames, and electrical and plumbing penetrations.

There are two types of foam-in-place insulation: closed-cell and open-cell. Both are typically made with polyurethane. With closed-cell foam, the high-density cells are closed and filled with a gas that helps the foam expand to fill the spaces around it. Closed-cell foam is the most effective, with an insulation value of around R-6.2 per inch of thickness.

U.S. Department of Energy Recommended*
Total R-Values for New Wood-Framed Houses

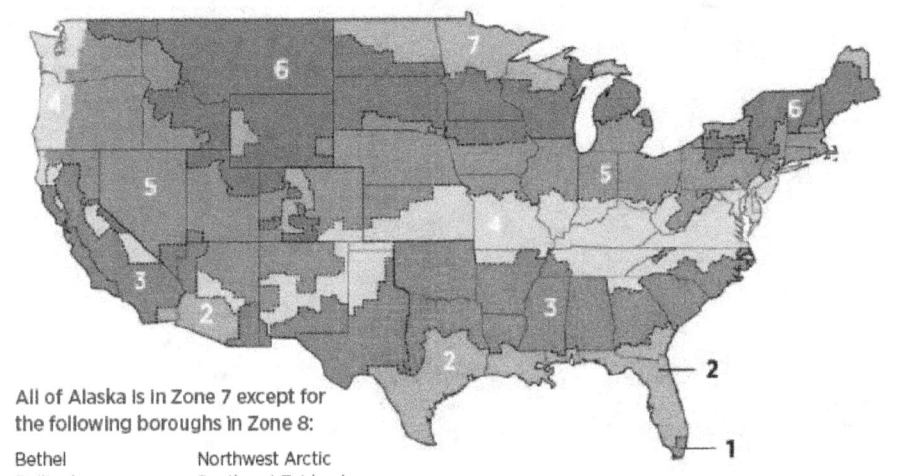

All of Alaska is in Zone 7 except for
the following boroughs in Zone 8:

Bethel
Dillingham
Fairbanks N. Star
Nome
North Slope

Northwest Arctic
Southeast Fairbanks
Wade Hampton
Yukon-Koyukuk

Zone 1 includes:
Hawaii, Guam, Puerto Rico
and the Virgin Islands

How Much Insulation Does My Home Need?
For insulation recommendations tailored to your
home, visit the DOE Zip Code Insulation Calculator
at *ornl.gov/~roofs/Zip/ZipHome.html*.

Zone	Gas	Heat Pump	Fuel Oil	Electric	Attic	Cathedral Ceiling	Cavity	Insulation Sheathing	Floor
1	•	•	•	•	R30 to R49	R22 to R38	R13 to R15	None	R13
2	•	•	•		R30 to R60	R22 to R38	R13 to R15	None	R13
				•	R30 to R60	R22 to R38	R13 to R15	None	R19 - R25
3	•	•	•		R30 to R60	R22 to R38	R13 to R15	None	R25
				•	R30 to R60	R22 to R38	R13 to R15	R2.5 to R5	R25
4	•	•	•		R38 to R60	R30 to R38	R13 to R15	R2.5 to R6	R25 - R30
				•	R38 to R60	R30 to R38	R13 to R15	R5 to R6	R25 - R30
5	•	•	•		R38 to R60	R30 to R38	R13 to R15	R2.5 to R6	R25 - R30
				•	R38 to R60	R30 to R60	R13 to R21	R5 to R6	R25 - R30
6	•	•	•	•	R49 to R60	R30 to R60	R13 to R21	R5 to R6	R25 - R30
7	•	•	•	•	R49 to R60	R30 to R60	R13 to R21	R5 to R6	R25 - R30
8	•	•	•	•	R49 to R60	R30 to R60	R13 to R21	R5 to R6	R25 - R30

* These recommendations are cost-effective levels of insulation based on the best available information on local fuel
and materials costs and weather conditions. Consequently, the levels may differ from current local building codes.

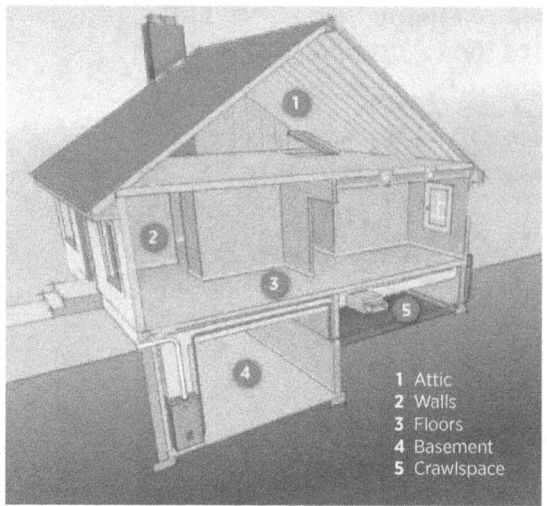

Where to Insulate

Adding insulation in the areas shown here may be the best way to improve your home's energy efficiency. Insulate either the attic floor or under the roof. Check with a contractor about crawl space or basement insulation.

1 Attic
2 Walls
3 Floors
4 Basement
5 Crawlspace

Open-cell foam cells are not as dense and are filled with air, which gives the insulation a spongy texture. Open-cell foam insulation value is around R-3.7 per inch of thickness.

The type of insulation you should choose depends on how you will use it and on your budget. While closed-cell foam has a greater R-value and provides stronger resistance against moisture and air leakage, the material is also much denser and is more expensive to install. Open-cell foam is lighter and less expensive but should not be used below ground level where it could absorb water. Consult a professional insulation installer to decide what type of insulation is best for you.

Insulation Tips

- Consider factors such as your climate, home design, and budget when selecting insulation for your home.
- Use higher R-value insulation, such as spray foam, on exterior walls and in cathedral ceilings to get more insulation with less thickness.
- Install attic air barriers such as wind baffles along the entire attic eave to

help ensure proper airflow from the soffit to the attic. Ventilation helps with moisture control and reducing summer cooling bills, but don't ventilate your attic if you have insulation on the underside of the roof. Ask a qualified contractor for recommendations.
- Be careful how close you place insulation next to a recessed light fixture—unless it is insulation contact (IC) rated—to avoid a fire hazard. See the Lighting section for more information about recessed lights.
- Follow the manufacturer's installation instructions, and wear the proper protective gear when installing insulation.

$ Long-Term Savings Tips

One of the most cost-effective ways to make your home more comfortable year-round is to add insulation to your attic, including the attic trap or access door, which is relatively easy. To find out if you have enough attic insulation, measure the thickness of the insulation.

If it is less than R-30 (11 inches of fiber glass or rock wool or 8 inches of cellulose), you could probably benefit by adding more.

If your attic has enough insulation and proper air sealing, and your home still feels drafty and cold in the winter or too warm in the summer, chances are you need to add insulation to the exterior walls. This is more expensive and usually requires a contractor, but it may be worth the cost—especially if you live in a very cold climate. If you replace the exterior siding on your home, consider adding insulation at the same time.

You may also need to add insulation to your crawl space or basement. Check with a professional contractor for recommendations.

New Construction and Additions

In most climates, you will save money and energy when you build a new home or addition if you install a combination of cavity insulation and insulative sheathing. Reduce exterior wall leaks by taping the joints of exterior sheathing and caulking and sealing exterior walls. Cavity insulation can be installed at levels up to R-15 in a 2 in. x 4 in. wall and up to R-21 in a 2 in. x 6 in. wall.

These help to reduce the energy that would otherwise be lost through the wood frame. The table on page 9 shows the recommended combinations. For more customized recommendations, see the ZIP Code Insulation Calculator at ornl.gov/~roofs/Zip/ZipHome.html.

Consider products that provide both insulation and structural support, such as structural insulated panels (SIPs), and masonry products like insulating concrete forms. Visit energysavers.gov for more information on structural insulation.

You should consider attic or roof radiant barriers (in hot climates), reflective insulation, and foundation insulation for new home construction. Check with your contractor for more information about these options.

Heating and Cooling

Heating and cooling your home uses more energy and costs more money than any other system in your home—typically making up about 54% of your utility bill.

No matter what kind of heating and cooling system you have in your house, you can save money and increase your comfort by properly maintaining and upgrading your equipment. But remember, an energy-efficient furnace alone will not have as great an impact on your energy bills as using the whole-house approach. By combining proper equipment maintenance and upgrades with recommended insulation, air sealing, and thermostat settings, you can cut your energy use for heating and cooling—and reduce environmental emissions—from 20%-50%.

Heating and Cooling Tips

- Set your programmable thermostat as low as is comfortable in the winter and as high as is comfortable in the summer, as well as when you're sleeping or away from home.
- Clean or replace filters on furnaces and air conditioners once a month or as recommended.
- Clean warm-air registers, baseboard heaters, and radiators as needed; make sure they're not blocked by furniture, carpeting, or drapes.

- Eliminate trapped air from hot-water radiators once or twice a season; if unsure about how to perform this task, contact a professional.
- Place heat-resistant radiator reflectors between exterior walls and the radiators.
- Turn off kitchen, bath, and other exhaust fans within 20 minutes after you are done cooking or bathing; when replacing exhaust fans, consider installing high-efficiency, low-noise models.
- During winter, keep the draperies and shades on your south-facing windows open during the day to allow the sunlight to enter your home and closed at night to reduce the chill you may feel from cold windows.

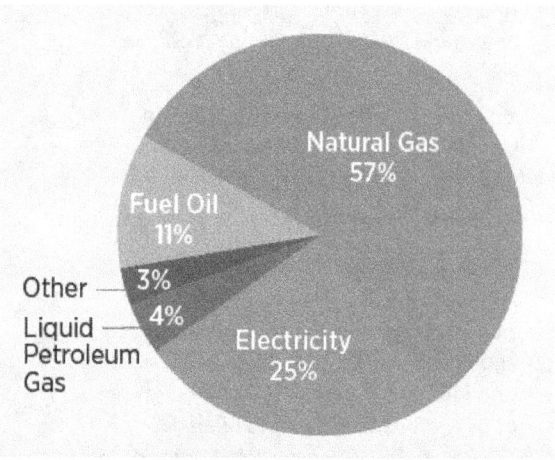

Household Heating Systems
Although several different types of fuels are available to heat our homes, more than half of us use natural gas.
Source: Buildings Energy Data Book 2010, 2.1.1 Residential Primary Energy Consumption, by Year and Fuel Type (Quadrillion Btu and Percent of Total)

- During summer, keep the window coverings closed during the day to block the sun's heat.

$ Long-Term Savings Tips

Select energy-efficient products when you buy new heating and cooling equipment. Your contractor should be able to give you energy fact sheets for different types, models, and designs to help you compare energy usage.

For furnaces, look for high Annual Fuel Utilization Efficiency (AFUE) ratings. The national minimum is 78% AFUE, but there are ENERGY STAR® models on the market that exceed 90% AFUE. For air conditioners, look for a high Seasonal Energy Efficiency Ratio (SEER). The current minimum is 13 SEER for central air conditioners. ENERGY STAR models are 14.5 SEER or more.

Air Ducts

Your air ducts are one of the most important systems in your home, and if the ducts are poorly sealed or insulated they are likely contributing to higher energy bills.

Your home's duct system is a branching network of tubes in the walls, floors, and ceilings; it carries the air from your home's furnace and central air conditioner to each room. Ducts are made of sheet metal, fiberglass, or other materials.

Ducts that leak heated air into unheated spaces can add hundreds of dollars a year to your heating and cooling bills. Insulating ducts that are in unconditioned spaces is usually very cost effective. If you are installing a new duct system, make sure it comes with insulation.

Sealing your ducts to prevent leaks is even more important if the ducts are located in an unconditioned area such as an attic or vented crawl space. If the supply ducts are leaking, heated or cooled air can be forced out of unsealed joints and lost. In addition, unconditioned air can be drawn into return ducts through unsealed joints.

Although minor duct repairs are easy to make, qualified professionals should seal and insulate ducts in unconditioned spaces to ensure the use of appropriate sealing materials.

Minor Duct Repair Tips

- Check your ducts for air leaks. First, look for sections that should be joined but have separated and then look for obvious holes.
- If you use tape to seal your ducts, avoid cloth-backed, rubber adhesive duct tape—it tends to fail quickly. Instead, use mastic, butyl tape, foil tape, or other heat-approved tapes. Look for tape with the Underwriters Laboratories (UL) logo.
- Remember that insulating ducts in the basement will make the basement colder. If both the ducts and the basement walls are not insulated, consider insulating both. Water pipes and drains in unconditioned spaces could freeze and burst if the heat ducts are fully insulated because there would be no heat source to prevent the space from freezing in cold weather. However, using an electric heating tape wrap on the pipes can prevent this. Check with a professional contractor.
- Hire a professional to install both supply and return registers in the basement rooms after converting your basement to a living area.
- Be sure a well-sealed vapor barrier exists on the outside of the insulation on cooling ducts to prevent moisture condensation.

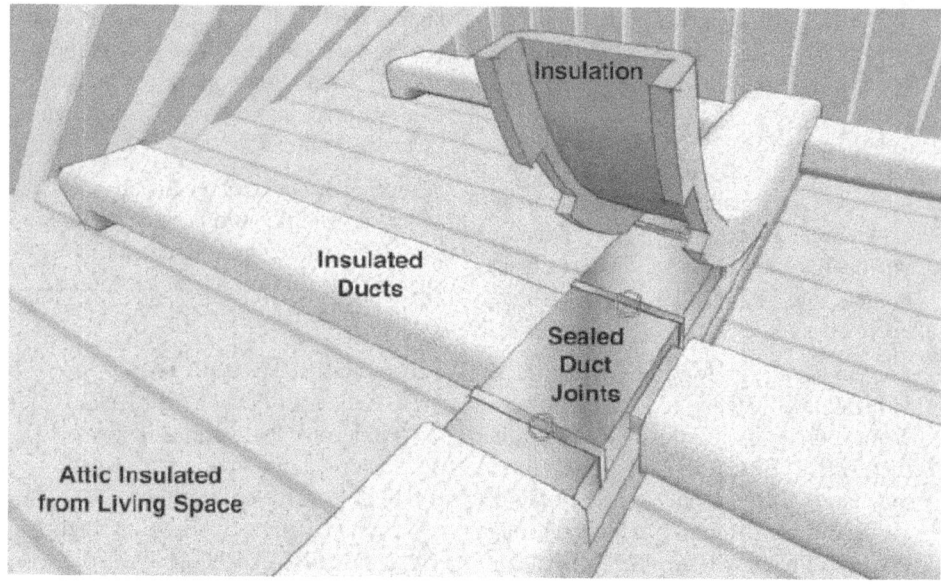

Air Ducts: Out of Sight, Out of Mind
The unsealed ducts in your attic and crawlspaces lose air, and uninsulated ducts lose heat—wasting energy and money.

- If you have a fuel-burning furnace, stove, or other appliance or an attached garage, install a carbon monoxide (CO) monitor to alert you to harmful CO levels.
- Be sure to get professional help when doing ductwork. A qualified professional should always perform changes and repairs to a duct system.

Install a Carbon Monoxide Detector

Carbon monoxide (CO) detectors are required in new buildings in many states. They are highly recommended in homes with fuel-burning appliances such as natural gas furnaces, stoves, ovens, water heaters, and space heaters. An alarm signals if CO reaches potentially dangerous levels.

Heat Pumps
Heat pumps are the most efficient form of electric heating in moderate climates, providing up to three times more heat than the energy they use. A heat pump can reduce your electricity use for heating by 30%-40% compared to electric resistance heating such as furnaces and baseboard heaters.

A heat pump does double duty as a central air conditioner by collecting the heat inside your house and pumping it outside.

There are three types of heat pumps: air-to-air, water source, and geothermal. They collect heat from the air, water, or ground outside your home and concentrate it for use inside.

Geothermal (or ground source) heat pumps have some major advantages. They can reduce energy use by 30%-60%, control humidity, are sturdy and reliable, and fit in a wide variety of homes.

Heat Pump Tips

- Do not set back the heat pump's thermostat manually if it causes the electric-resistance heating to come on. This type of heating, which is often used as a backup to the heat pump, is more expensive.
- Install or have a professional install a programmable thermostat with multistage functions suitable for a heat pump.
- Clean or change filters once a month or as needed, and maintain the system according to manufacturer's instructions.

$ Long-Term Savings Tip

If you heat your home with electricity and live in a moderate climate, consider an energy-efficient heat pump system to reduce your energy consumption.

Passive Solar Heating and Cooling

Using passive solar design to heat and cool your home can be both environmentally friendly and cost effective. In many cases, your heating costs can be reduced to less than half the cost of heating a typical home.

Passive solar design can also help lower your cooling costs. Passive solar cooling techniques include carefully designed overhangs and using reflective coatings on windows, exterior walls, and roofs. Newer techniques include placing large, insulated windows on south-facing walls and putting thermal mass, such as a concrete slab floor or a heat-absorbing wall, close to the windows.

A passive solar house requires careful design and siting, which vary by local climate conditions. If you are considering passive solar design for a new home or a major remodel, consult an architect familiar with passive solar techniques.

Passive Solar Tips

- Keep all south-facing glass clean.
- Make sure that objects do not block sunlight on concrete slab floors or heat-absorbing walls.

Natural Gas and Oil Heating

If you plan to buy a new heating system, ask your local utility or state energy office about the latest technologies on the market. For example, many newer models have designs for burners and heat exchangers that are more efficient during operation and cut heat loss when the equipment is off.

Consider a sealed-combustion furnace— they are safer and more efficient.

$ Long-Term Savings Tip

Install a new energy-efficient furnace to save money over the long term. Look for the ENERGY STAR and EnergyGuide labels to compare efficiency and ensure quality.

Programmable Thermostats

You can save as much as 10% a year on heating and cooling by simply turning your thermostat back 7°-10°F for 8 hours a day from where you would normally set. (If you have a heat pump, don't do this without a programmable thermostat). You can do this automatically by using a programmable thermostat and scheduling the times you turn on the heating or air conditioning. As a result, the equipment doesn't operate as much when you are asleep or not at home.

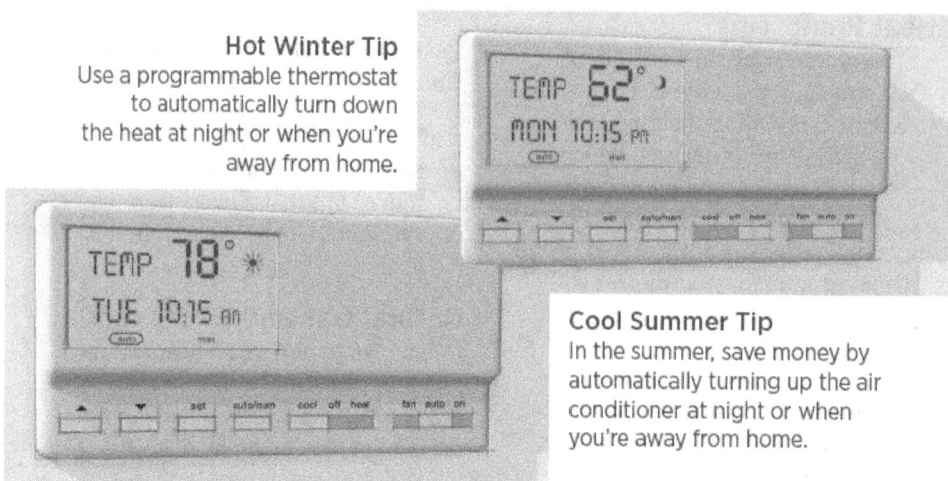

Programmable thermostats can store multiple daily settings (six or more temperature settings a day) that you can manually override without affecting the rest of the daily or weekly program.

Air Conditioners

Buying a bigger room air conditioner won't necessarily make you feel more comfortable during the hot summer months. In fact, a room air conditioner that's too big for the area it is supposed to cool will perform less efficiently and less effectively than a smaller, properly sized unit. Central air-conditioning systems need to be sized by professionals.

If you have a central air system in your home, set the fan to shut off at the same time as the compressor, which is usually done by setting the "auto" mode on the fan setting. In other words, don't use the system's central fan to provide air circulation—use circulating fans in individual rooms.

Instead of air-conditioning, consider installing a whole-house fan. Whole-house fans work in many climates and

help cool your home by pulling cool air through the house and exhausting warm air through the attic. Use the fan most effectively to cool down your house during cooler times of the day: your home will stay cooler through the hotter times of the day without using the fan.

Cooling Tips

• Set your thermostat at as high a temperature as comfortably possible in the summer, and ensure humidity control if needed. The smaller the difference between the indoor and outdoor temperatures, the lower your overall cooling bill will be.

• Avoid setting your thermostat at a colder setting than normal when you turn on your air conditioner. It will not cool your home any faster and could result in excessive cooling and, therefore, unnecessary expense.

• Consider using an interior fan along with your window air conditioner to spread the cooled air through your home without greatly increasing your power use.

Buildings and Trees—Natural Partners
Deciduous trees planted on the south and west sides will help keep your house cool in the summer and allow sun to shine through the windows in the winter.

- Avoid placing appliances that give off heat such as lamps or TVs near a thermostat.

$ Long-Term Savings Tips

If your air conditioner is old, consider buying an energy-efficient model. Look for the ENERGY STAR and EnergyGuide labels—qualified room air conditioners are 10% more efficient, and qualified central units are about 14% more efficient than standard models.

Consider installing a whole-house fan or evaporative cooler if appropriate for your climate. Check out energysavers.gov for more information on efficient cooling.

Cool Roofs

If you've ever stood on a roof on a hot summer day, you know how hot it can get. The heat from your roof makes your air conditioner work even harder to keep your home cool.

If you are building a new home, decide during planning whether you want a cool roof, and if you want to convert an existing roof, you can:

- Retrofit the roof with specialized heat-reflective material.
- Re-cover the roof with a new waterproofing surface (such as tile coating).
- Replace the roof with a cool one.

A cool roof uses material that is designed to reflect more sunlight and absorb less heat than a standard roof. Cool roofs can be made of a highly reflective type of paint, a sheet covering, or highly reflective tiles or shingles.

By installing a cool roof, you can lower the temperature of your roof by up to 50°F and save energy and money by using less air conditioning. Cool roofs make spaces like garages or covered patios more comfortable.

As cool roofs become more popular, communities will benefit from fewer power plant emissions and less demand for new power plants. Cool roofs can lower outside air temperatures, reducing heat islands in urban areas.

Nearly any type of home can benefit from a cool roof, but consider climate and other factors before you decide to install one. Visit energysavers.gov to learn more about cool roofs.

Green Roofs

You may also consider installing a green roof. Green roofs are ideal for urban buildings with flat or shallow-pit roofs, and can include anything from basic plant cover to a garden. The primary reasons for using this type of roof include managing storm water and enjoying a rooftop open space. Green roofs also provide insulation, lower the need for heating and cooling, and can reduce the urban heat island effect. This roof type can be much more expensive to implement than other efficient roof options, so you should carefully assess your property and consult a professional before deciding to install a green roof.

Visit the Green Roofs for Healthy Cities industry website at greenroofs.org for more information.

Landscaping

Landscaping is a natural and beautiful way to keep your home cool in summer and reduce your energy bills. A well-placed tree, shrub, or vine can deliver effective shade, act as a windbreak, and reduce your energy bills—see landscaping illustration. Carefully positioned trees can save up to 25% of the energy a typical household uses.[1] Research shows that summer day-time air temperatures can be 3°-6° cooler in tree-shaded neighborhoods than in treeless areas.[2]

A lattice or trellis with climbing vines or a planter box with trailing vines shades the home while admitting cooling breezes to the shaded area.

Water Heating

Water heating is the second largest energy expense in your home. It typically accounts for about 18% of your utility bill.

There are four ways to cut your water heating bills: use less hot water, turn down the thermostat on your water heater, insulate your water heater, or buy a new, more efficient model.

Water Heating Tips

- Install aerating, low-flow faucets and showerheads.
- Repair leaky faucets promptly; a leaky faucet wastes gallons of water in a short period of time.
- Set the thermostat on your water heater to 120°F to get comfortable hot water for most uses.
- Insulate your electric hot-water storage tank but be careful not to cover the thermostat. Follow the manufacturer's recommendations.
- Insulate your natural gas or oil hot-water storage tank but be careful not to cover the water heater's top, bottom, thermostat, or burner compartment. Follow the manufacturer's recommendations; when in doubt, get professional help.
- Insulate the first 6 feet of the hot and cold water pipes connected to the water heater.

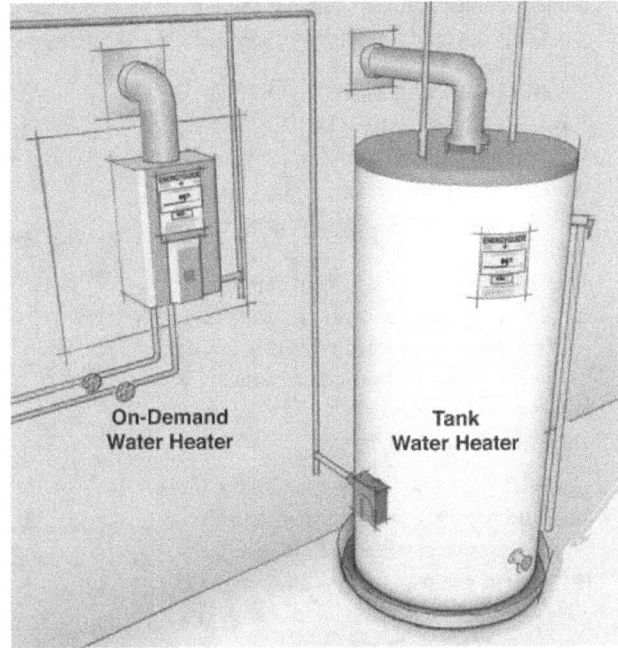

On-Demand Water Heater

Tank Water Heater

Keep Your Energy Bills Out of Hot Water
Insulate your water heater to save energy and money, or choose an on-demand hot water heater to save even more.

- If you are in the market for a new dishwasher or clothes washer, consider buying an efficient, water-saving ENERGY STAR® model to reduce hot water use. See the Appliances section for more information.
- Install heat traps on the hot and cold pipes at the water heater to prevent heat loss. Most new water heaters have built-in heat traps.
- Drain a quart of water from your water tank every 3 months to remove sediment that impedes heat transfer and lowers the efficiency of your heater. Follow the manufacturer's directions.

Although most water heaters last 10-15 years, it's best to start shopping now for a new one if yours is more than 7 years old. Doing some research before your heater fails will enable you to select one that most appropriately meets your needs.

$ Long-Term Savings Tips

Buy a new energy-efficient water heater. While it may cost more initially than a standard water heater, the energy savings will continue during the lifetime of the appliance. Look for the ENERGY STAR® and EnergyGuide labels. You can find the ENERGY STAR label on efficient water heaters in the following categories: high efficiency gas non-condensing, gas condensing, electric heat pump, gas tankless, and solar.

Consider natural gas on-demand or tankless water heaters, which heat water directly without using a storage tank. Researchers have found energy savings can be up to 30% compared with a standard natural gas storage tank water heater.[3]

Consider installing a drain-water waste heat recovery system. Drain-water, or greywater, heat recovery systems capture the energy from waste hot water—such as showers and dishwashers—to preheat cold water entering the water heater or going to other water fixtures. Energy savings vary depending on individual household usage.

Heat pump water heaters can be very cost effective in some areas. They typically use 50% less electricity to heat water than conventional electric water heaters. If your water heater is located in your basement, it will also provide dehumidification in the summer months. However, this technology can pose some installation challenges, so you should consult with an installer before you purchase one. For more information see energysavers.gov.

Activity	Gallons per Use
Clothes washer	7
Shower	10
Automatic dishwasher	6
Kitchen faucet flow	2 per minute
Bathroom faucet flow	.05 per minute
Total daily average	64

Average Hot Water Usage
Faucets and appliances can use a lot of hot water, which costs you money. Look for ways to heat your water more efficiently and use less. *Source: Federal Energy Management Program Energy Cost Calculator, March 2010*

Solar Water Heaters

If you heat water with electricity, have high electric rates, and have an unshaded, south-facing location (such as a roof) on your property, consider installing a solar water heater. The solar units are environmentally friendly and you can have them installed on your roof to blend with the architecture of your house.

Solar water heating systems are also good for the environment. Solar water heaters avoid the greenhouse gas emissions associated with electricity production. When shopping for a solar water heater, look for the ENERGY STAR label and for systems certified by the Solar Rating and Certification Corporation or the Florida Solar Energy Center.

$ Long-Term Savings Tip

Visit the Database of State Incentives for Renewables & Efficiency website (dsireusa.org) to see if you qualify for tax credits or rebates for buying a solar water heater.

Windows

Windows can be one of your home's most attractive features. Windows provide views, daylighting, ventilation, and heat from the sun in the winter. Unfortunately, they can also account for 10%-25% of your heating bill by letting heat out.

During the summer, your air conditioner must work harder to cool hot air from sunny windows. Install ENERGY STAR®-qualified windows and use curtains and shade to give your air conditioner and energy bill a break.

If your home has single-pane windows, consider replacing them with double-pane windows with high-performance glass—low-e or spectrally selective coatings. In colder climates, select gas-filled windows with low-e coatings to reduce heat loss. In warmer climates, select windows with spectrally selective coatings to reduce heat gain.

If you decide not to replace your windows, consider following these tips to improve their performance.

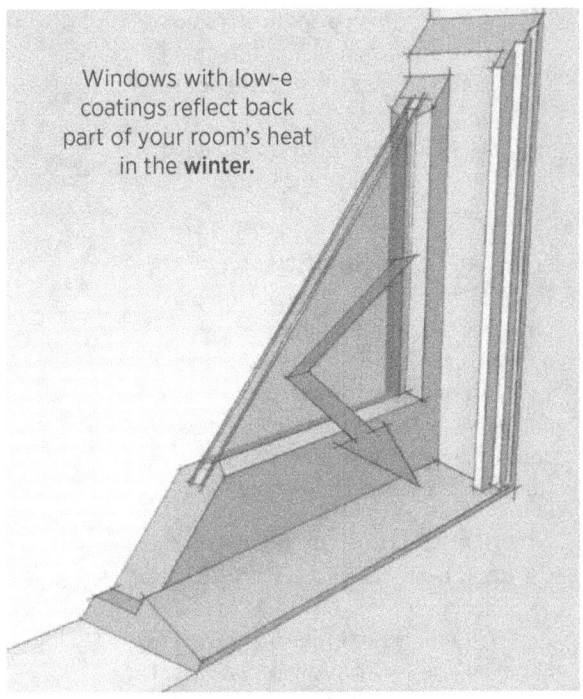

Windows with low-e coatings reflect back part of your room's heat in the **winter.**

Cold-Climate Windows Keep Heat In
Double-pane windows with low-e coating on the glass reflect heat back into the room during the winter months.

Cold Weather Window Tips

- Use a heavy-duty, clear plastic sheet on a frame or tape clear plastic film to the inside of your window frames to reduce drafts.
- Install tight-fitting, insulating window shades on windows that feel drafty after weatherizing.
- Close your curtains and shades at night to protect against cold drafts; open them during the day to let in warming sunlight.
- Install exterior or interior storm windows, which can reduce heat loss through the windows by 25%-50%. They should have weatherstripping at all movable joints; be made of strong, durable materials; and have interlocking or overlapping joints.
- Repair and weatherize your current storm windows, if necessary.

Warm Weather Window Tips

- Install white window shades, drapes, or blinds to reflect heat away from the house.
- Close curtains on south- and west-facing windows during the day.
- Install awnings on south- and west-facing windows.
- Apply sun-control or other reflective films on south-facing windows to reduce solar heat gain.

$ Long-Term Savings Tip

Installing high-performance windows will improve your home's energy performance. While it may take many years for new windows to pay off in energy savings, the benefits of added comfort, improved aesthetics, and functionality can offset the cost.

Shopping Tips for Windows

- Look for the ENERGY STAR® label.
- Check with local utilities to see what rebates or other incentives are available for window replacement.
- Choose high-performance windows that have at least two panes of glass and a low-e coating.
- Choose a low U-factor for better insulation in colder climates; the U-factor is the rate at which a window, door, or skylight conducts non-solar heat flow.
- Look for a low solar heat gain coefficient (SHGC)—this is a measure of solar radiation admitted through a window, door, or skylight. Low SHGCs reduce heat gain in warm climates.
- Select windows with both low U-factors and low SHGCs to maximize energy savings in temperate climates with both cold and hot seasons.

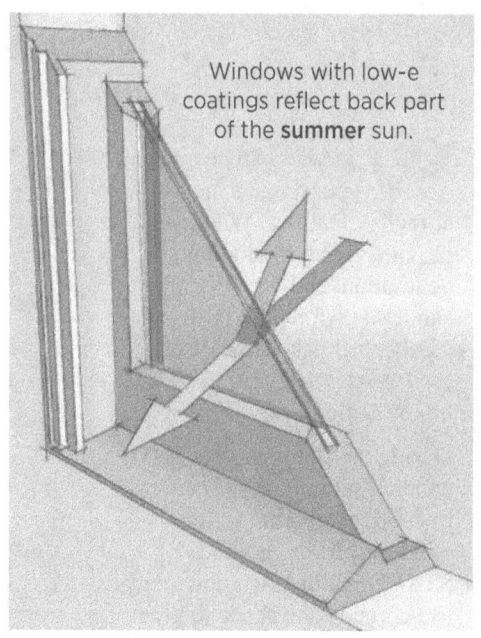

Windows with low-e coatings reflect back part of the **summer** sun.

Warm-Climate Windows Keep Heat Out
In the summertime, the sun shining through your windows heats up the room. Windows with low-e coatings on the glass reflect some of the sunlight, keeping your rooms cooler.

- Look for whole-unit U-factors and SHGCs, rather than center-of-glass (COG) U-factors and SHGCs. Whole-unit numbers more accurately reflect the energy performance of the entire product.
- Have your windows installed by trained professionals according to manufacturer's instructions; otherwise, your warranty may be void.
- Consider windows with impact-resistant glass if you live along a coast or in areas with flying debris from storms.

Lighting

An average household dedicates about 6% of its energy budget to lighting. Switching to energy-efficient lighting is one of the fastest ways to cut your energy bills. Timers and motion sensors save you even more money by reducing the amount of time lights are on but not being used.

Indoor Lighting

You have many choices in energy-efficient lighting. The most popular light bulbs available are halogen incandescents, compact fluorescent lamps (CFLs), and light-emitting diodes (LEDs). Although they can initially cost more than traditional incandescent bulbs, over their lifetime they save you money because they use less electricity.

Energy-Saving (also called Halogen) Incandescent Lighting

Halogen incandescent light bulbs are simply energy-efficient incandescent bulbs and can last up to three times longer than traditional incandescent light bulbs. Halogen incandescents come in a wide range of shapes and colors and can be used with dimmers.

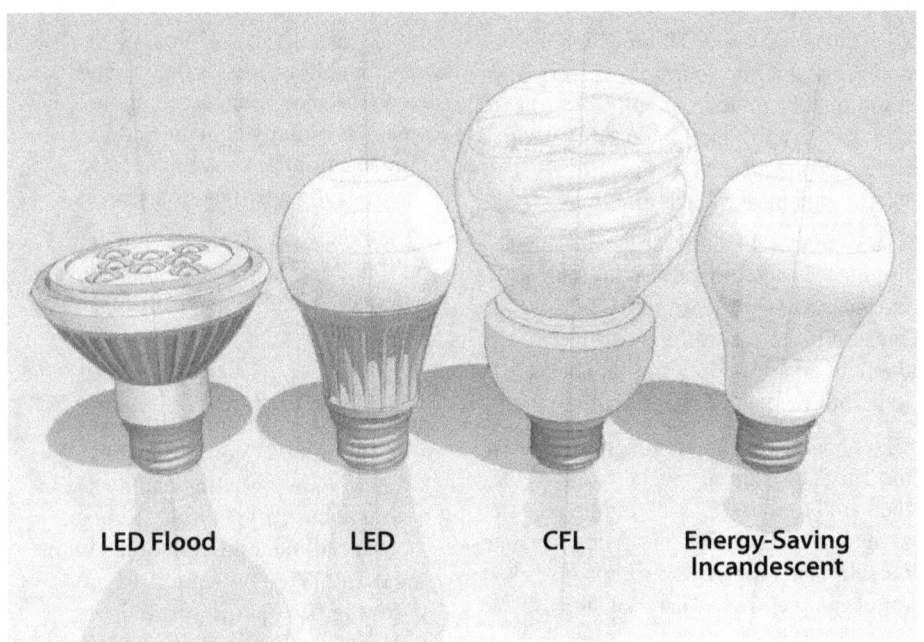

LED Flood   LED   CFL   Energy-Saving
                                             Incandescent

Lighting Choices Save You Money
Energy-efficient light bulbs are available in a wide variety of sizes and shapes.

CFL Bulbs

ENERGY STAR®-qualified CFLs use about 75% less energy and last up to 10 times longer than traditional incandescents.

CFL Lighting

CFL bulbs last about 10 times longer and use about one-fourth the energy of traditional incandescent bulbs. A typical CFL can pay for itself in energy savings in less than 9 months and continue to save you money each month.

You can buy CFLs that offer the same brightness and colors as traditional incandescent bulbs. Some CFLs are encased in a cover to further diffuse the light and provide a similar shape to traditional incandescent bulbs.

CFLs contain a very small amount of mercury and require special handling if they are broken. CFLs should be recycled at the end of their lifespan. Many retailers recycle CFLs for free. Visit epa.gov/cfl for cleanup and safe disposal steps.

LED Lighting

LED bulbs are rapidly expanding in household use. ENERGY STAR-qualified LEDs use only about 20%-25% of the

LEDs: A New Kind of Light

LED bulbs offer similar light quality to traditional incandescents, last 25 times as long, and use even less energy than CFLs. Choose ENERGY STAR-qualified LEDs for the highest quality and energy savings.

energy and last up to 25 times longer than traditional incandescent bulbs. They come in a variety of colors, and some are dimmable or offer convenient features such as daylight and motion sensors.

In addition to standard screw-in bulbs, you'll find LEDs in desk lamps, kitchen under-cabinet lighting, and even holiday light strings.

Indoor Lighting Tips

- Replacing 15 inefficient incandescent bulbs in your home with energy-saving bulbs could save you about $50 per year. Replace your old incandescent bulbs with ENERGY STAR-qualified bulbs for the best quality in savings.
- Visit energystar.gov to find the right light bulbs for your fixtures. They are available in sizes and shapes to

fit in almost any fixture and provide the greatest savings in fixtures that are on for a long time each day.

- When remodeling, look for recessed light fixtures or "cans" which are rated for contact with insulation and are air tight (ICAT rated).
- When replacing incandescent bulbs from recessed light fixtures, use energy-efficient bulbs that are rated for that purpose. For example, the heat buildup in downlights will significantly shorten the life of spiral CFLs.
- Consider purchasing ENERGY STAR-qualified fixtures. They are available in many styles, distribute light more efficiently and evenly than standard fixtures, and some offer convenient features such as dimming.
- Controls such as timers and photo-cells save electricity by turning lights off when not in use. Dimmers save electricity when used to lower light levels. Be sure to select products that are compatible with the energy-efficient bulbs you want to use.
- Keep your curtains or shades open to use daylighting instead of turning on lights. For more privacy, use light-colored, loose-weave curtains to allow daylight into the room. Also, decorate with lighter colors that reflect daylight.

Outdoor Lighting

Many homeowners use outdoor lighting for decoration and security. A variety of products are available from low-voltage pathway lighting to motion-detector floodlights.

LEDs work well indoors and outdoors because of their durability and perfor-

Recycle Your Old CFLs

CFLs contain a small amount of mercury sealed within the glass tubing, and must be recycled. Many retailers offer free recycling services, and some municipalities have special recycling programs.

mance in cold environments. Look for LED products such as pathway lights, step lights, and porch lights for outdoor use. You can also find solar powered outdoor lighting.

Outdoor Lighting Tips

- Because outdoor lights are usually left on a long time, using CFLs or LEDs in these fixtures will save a lot of energy. Most bare spiral CFLs can be used in enclosed fixtures that protect them from the weather.
- CFLs and LEDs are available as flood lights. These models have been tested to withstand the rain and snow so they can be used in exposed fixtures.
- Look for ENERGY STAR-qualified fixtures that are designed for outdoor use and come with features like automatic daylight shut-off and motion sensors.

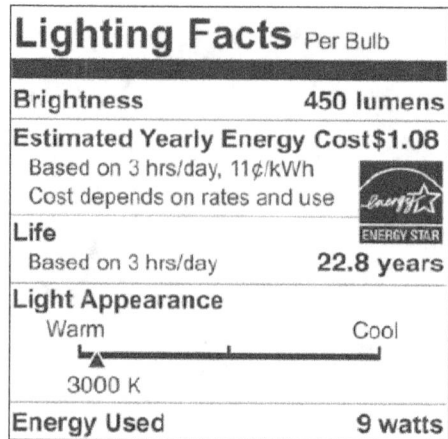

Lighting Facts Per Bulb

Brightness	**450 lumens**
Estimated Yearly Energy Cost	**$1.08**
Based on 3 hrs/day, 11¢/kWh	
Cost depends on rates and use	
Life	
Based on 3 hrs/day	**22.8 years**
Light Appearance	
Warm	Cool
3000 K	
Energy Used	**9 watts**

The Lighting Facts Label

You'll find a new label on light bulb packages starting in 2012: the Lighting Facts label. The Federal Trade Commission is requiring the label on all light bulb packages to help consumers easily compare energy-efficient light bulbs. The label includes:

- Brightness, measured in lumens
- Estimated yearly energy cost (similar to the EnergyGuide label)
- Lifespan
- Light appearance (from warm to cool)
- Energy used, measured in watts.

Like the helpful nutrition label on food products, the Lighting Facts label will help you to understand exactly what you are buying and to buy the light bulbs that are right for you.

New Lighting Standards in 2012

Beginning in 2012, the common light bulbs we use will be required to be about 25% more energy efficient to meet the new efficiency standards of the bipartisan Energy Independence and Security Act of 2007 (EISA 2007).

As of January 1, 2012, traditional 100 W incandescent light bulbs will not meet the standards and will no longer be available. Similar standards will take effect for traditional 75 W incandescent bulbs as of January 1, 2013, and traditional 40 W and 60 W incandescent bulbs as of January 1, 2014. However, you have many lighting options that are EISA-compliant and will save you money.

Lumens: A New Way to Shop for Light

In the past, we bought light bulbs based on how much energy, or watts, they use. Wouldn't it make more sense to buy lights based on how much light they provide?

When you're shopping for light bulbs, you can choose your next light bu b for the brightness you want by comparing lumens instead of watts. A **lumen** is a measure of the amount of **brightness** of a light bu b—the higher the number of lumens, the brighter the light bulb.

If you're replacing an inefficient 100W bulb, look for an energy-saving bulb that puts out about 1600 lumens. To replace a 60 W equivalent, look for a bulb with about 800 lumens.

So when you're looking for a new bulb, look for lumens—or how bright the bulb is. Now that's a pretty bright idea!

Appliances

Appliances account for about 13% of your household's energy costs, with refrigeration, cooking, and laundry at the top of the list.

When you're shopping for appliances, think of two price tags. The first one covers the purchase price—think of it as a down payment. The second price tag is the cost of operating the appliance during its lifetime. You'll be paying on that second price tag every month with your utility bill for the next 10 to 20 years, depending on the appliance. Refrigerators last an average of 12 years; clothes washers about 11 years; dishwashers about 10 years; and room air conditioners last about 9 years.

When you shop for a new appliance, look for the ENERGY STAR® label. ENERGY STAR products usually exceed minimum federal standards by a substantial amount.

To help you figure out whether an appliance is energy efficient, the federal government requires most appliances to display the bright yellow and black EnergyGuide label. Although these labels will not show you which appliance is the most efficient on the market, they will show you the annual energy consumption and operating cost for each appliance so you can compare them yourself.

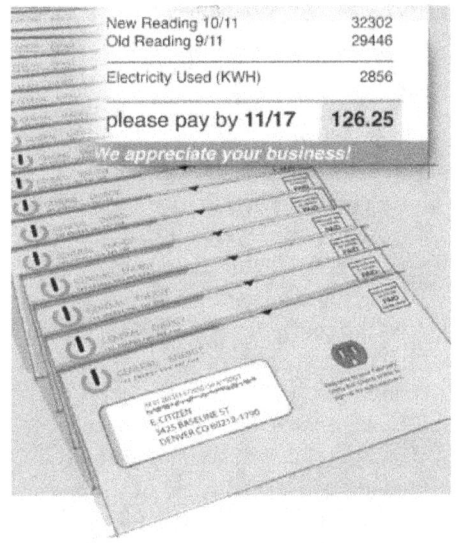

What's the Real Cost?
Every appliance has two price tags—the purchase price and the operating cost. Consider both when buying a new appliance.

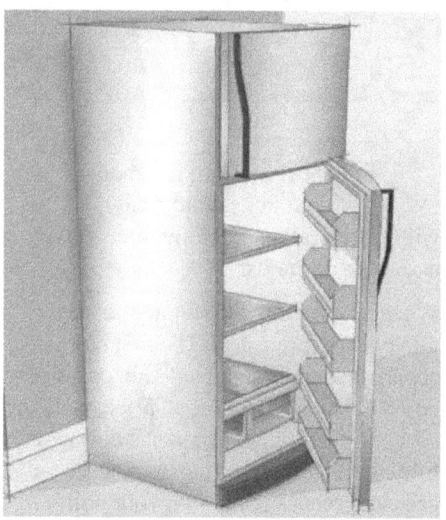

ENERGY STAR® Refrigerators Are Cool!
ENERGY STAR-qualified refrigerators are 20% more energy efficient than non-qualified models. Models with top-mounted freezers use 10%–25% less energy than side-by-side or bottom-mount units.

Dishwashers

Most of the energy used by a dishwasher is for water heating. The EnergyGuide label estimates how much power is needed per year to run the appliance and to heat the water based on the yearly cost of natural gas and electric water heating.

Dishwasher Water-Saving Tips

- Check the manual that came with your dishwasher for the manufacturer's recommendations on water temperature; many have internal heating elements that allow you to set the water heater in your home to a lower temperature (120°F).
- Scrape, don't rinse, off large food pieces and bones. Soaking or pre-washing is generally only recommended in cases of burned- or dried-on food.
- Be sure your dishwasher is full (not overloaded) when you run it.
- Avoid using the "rinse hold" on your machine for just a few soiled dishes. It uses 3-7 gallons of hot water each use.

- Let your dishes air dry; if you don't have an automatic air-dry switch, turn off the control knob after the final rinse and prop the door open slightly so the dishes will dry faster.

$ Long-Term Savings Tip

When shopping for a new dishwasher, look for the ENERGY STAR label to find one that uses less water and energy than required by federal standards. They are required to use 5.8 gallons of water per cycle or less—older dishwashers purchased before 1994 use more than 10 gallons of water per cycle.

Smart Appliances

Some manufacturers are now offering "smart" appliances—appliances that can be connected to smart electric meters or home energy management systems

How to Read the EnergyGuide Label

The EnergyGuide label is required to be placed on all appliances by the manufacturers. The label provides information about energy consumption, and shows you how much energy an appliance uses compared with similar models. Keep in mind that the numbers are averages: actual costs will differ somewhat depending on how you use them.

1. Maker, model number, and size of the appliance.

2. Estimated yearly operating cost (based on the national average cost of electricity), and the range of operating costs for similar models.

3. The ENERGY STAR® logo indicates that this model meets strict criteria for energy efficiency.

4. Estimated yearly electricity consumption.

5. Key features of the appliance and the similar models that make up the cost comparison range.

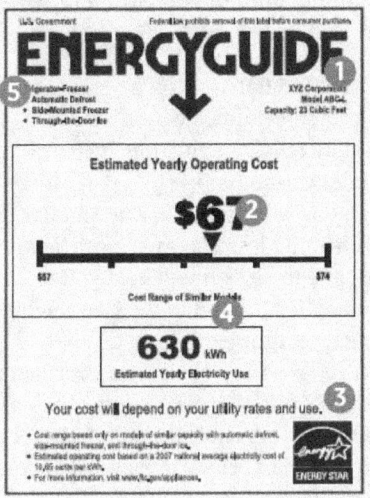

The ENERGY STAR® Logo

The ENERGY STAR logo is on all qualified products that meet specific standards for energy efficiency. ENERGY STAR-qualified products exceed the federal minimum standards for efficiency and quality—sometimes significantly. Look for the label on appliances, electronics, water heaters, windows, and other products that consume energy in your home.

to help you shift your electricity use to off-peak hours. Air conditioners, refrigerators, dishwashers, and other appliances may be available as smart appliances.

Smart appliances don't just turn off during times of peak electricity demand—instead, they use subtle ways to shift energy use. You might not even be aware of it. For example, your air conditioner may run slightly less often. Or your refrigerator might delay it's defrost cycle until the middle of the night. If your utility charges lower rates for electricity at night, also called time-based rates, you could save on your utility bill.

Such changes may be unnoticeable to you, but could add up to significant savings for your utility—savings that can be shared with you. Your utility provider can tell you more about the availability of smart grid technologies and time-based electricity rates in your area and how they can benefit you.

Refrigerators

The EnergyGuide label on new refrigerators tells you how much electricity in kilowatt-hours (kWh) a particular model uses in one year. The smaller the number, the less energy the refrigerator uses and the less it will cost you to operate. In addition to the EnergyGuide label, don't forget to look for the ENERGY STAR label. A new refrigerator with an ENERGY STAR label uses at least 20% less energy than required by current federal standards and 40% less energy than the conventional models sold in 2001.

Refrigerator-Freezer Energy Tips

- Don't keep your refrigerator or freezer too cold. Recommended temperatures are 37°-40°F for the fresh food compartment and 5°F for the freezer section. If you have a separate freezer for long-term storage, it should be kept at 0°F.
- Check the refrigerator temperature by placing an appliance thermometer in a glass of water in the center of the refrigerator. Read it after 24 hours. Check the freezer temperature by placing a thermometer between frozen packages. Read it after 24 hours.
- Make sure your refrigerator door seals are airtight. Test them by closing the door over a piece of

Save Energy and More with ENERGY STAR
ENERGY STAR clothes washers use 50% less energy to wash clothes than standard washing machines.

paper or a dollar bill so it is half in and half out of the refrigerator. If you can pull the paper or bill out easily, the latch may need adjustment, the seal may need replacing, or you may consider buying a new unit.
- Cover liquids and wrap foods stored in the refrigerator. Uncovered foods release moisture and make the compressor work harder.
- Regularly defrost manual-defrost freezers and refrigerators; frost buildup decreases the energy efficiency of the unit. Don't allow frost to build up more than one-quarter of an inch.

$ Long-Term Savings Tip

Look for the ENERGY STAR label when buying a new refrigerator. Select a new refrigerator that is the right size for your household. Top freezer models are more energy efficient than side-by-side models. Features like icemakers and water dispensers, while convenient, do use more energy.

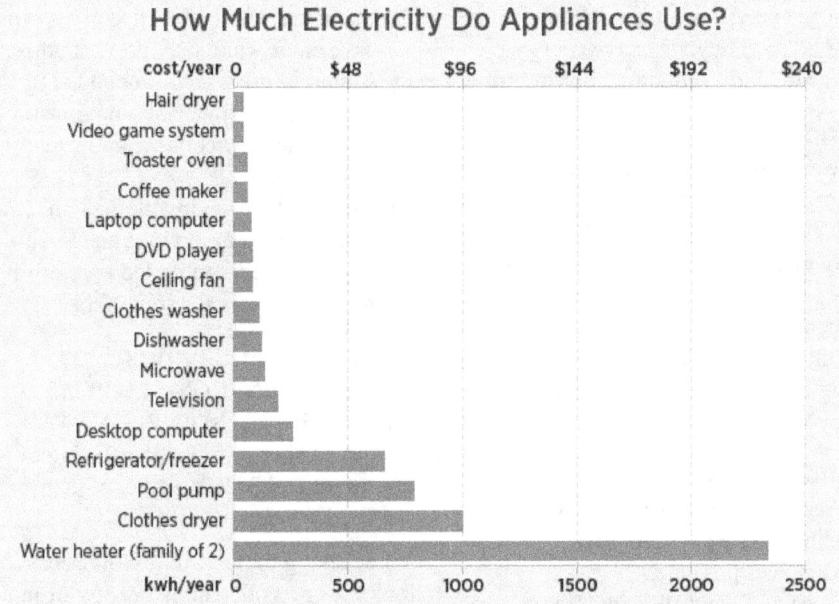

How Much Electricity Do Appliances Use?

This chart shows how much energy a typical appliance uses per year and its corresponding cost based on national averages. For example, a refrigerator uses almost five times the electricity the average television uses. Visit energysavers.gov for instructions on calculating the electrical use of your appliances. *Source: Buildings Energy Data Book 2010, 2.1.16 Operating Characteristics of Electric Appliances in the Residential Sector*

Other Energy-Saving Kitchen Tips

- Place the faucet lever on the kitchen sink in the cold position when using small amounts of water; placing the lever in the hot position draws hot water even though it may never reach the faucet.
- Look for a natural gas oven or range with an automatic, electric ignition system, which saves gas since a pilot light is not burning continuously.
- Look for blue flames in natural gas appliances; yellow flames indicate the gas is burning inefficiently and an adjustment may be needed. If you see yellow flames, consult the manufacturer or your local utility.

- Keep range-top burners and reflectors clean; they will reflect the heat better, and you will save energy.
- Use a covered kettle or pan or electric kettle to boil water; it's faster and uses less energy.
- Match the size of the pan to the heating element.
- Use small electric pans, toaster ovens, or convection ovens for small meals rather than your large stove or oven. A toaster or convection oven uses one-third to one-half as much energy as a full-sized oven.

- Use pressure cookers and microwave ovens whenever it is convenient to do so. They will save energy by significantly reducing cooking time.

Laundry

There are two ways to reduce the amount of energy used for washing clothes—use less water and use cooler water. Unless you're dealing with oily stains, the warm or cold water setting on your machine will generally do a good job of cleaning your clothes. Switching your temperature setting from hot to warm can cut a load's energy use in half.

Laundry Tips

- Wash your clothes in cold water using cold-water detergents whenever possible.
- Wash and dry full loads. If you are washing a small load, use the appropriate water-level setting.
- Dry towels and heavier cottons in a separate load from lighter-weight clothes.
- Don't over-dry your clothes. If your machine has a moisture sensor, use it.
- Clean the lint screen in the dryer after every load to improve air circulation and prevent fire hazards.
- Periodically, use the long nozzle tip on your vacuum cleaner to remove the lint that collects below the lint screen in the lint screen slot of your clothes dryer.
- Use the cool-down cycle to allow the clothes to finish drying with the heat remaining in the dryer.

- Periodically inspect your dryer vent to ensure it is not blocked. This will save energy and may prevent a fire. Manufacturers recommend using rigid venting material—not plastic vents that may collapse and cause blockages.
- Consider air-drying clothes on clothes lines or drying racks. Air drying is recommended by clothing manufacturers for some fabrics.

$ Long-Term Savings Tips

Look for the ENERGY STAR® and EnergyGuide labels. ENERGY STAR clothes washers clean clothes using 50% less water and 37% less energy than standard washers.

When shopping for a new clothes dryer, look for one with a moisture sensor that automatically shuts off the machine when your clothes are dry. Not only will this save energy, it will save the wear and tear on your clothes caused by over-drying.

ENERGY STAR does not label clothes dryers because most of them use similar amounts of energy.

Home Office and Electronics

Many people work from home at least one day per week. Working from home saves energy and time by cutting out the commute, but it may increase your home energy bills unless you use energy-saving office equipment.

ENERGY STAR-labeled office equipment is widely available. It can provide dramatic energy savings— as much as 90% savings for some products. Overall, ENERGY STAR-labeled office products use about half the electricity of standard equipment. Find ENERGY STAR products and standards at energystar.gov.

Home Office Tips

- Selecting energy-efficient office equipment and turning off machines when they are not in use can result in significant energy savings.
- Using an ENERGY STAR-labeled computer can save 30%-65% energy than computers without this designation, depending on usage.
- Spending a large portion of time in low-power mode not only saves energy but helps equipment run cooler and last longer.
- Putting your laptop AC adapter on a power strip that can be turned off (or will turn off automatically) can maximize savings; the transformer in the AC adapter draws power continuously, even when the laptop is not plugged into the adapter.

- Using the power management settings on computers and monitors can cause significant savings.
- It is a common misperception that screen savers reduce a monitor's energy use. Use automatic switching to sleep mode or simply turn it off.

Keep Your Home Office Efficient with ENERGY STAR
Laptops are far more efficient than desktop computers, especially ENERGY STAR qualified models.

- Another misperception, carried over from the days of older mainframe computers, is that equipment lasts longer if it is never turned off.

$ Long-Term Savings Tip

Consider buying a laptop for your next computer upgrade; laptops use much less energy than desktop computers.

Home Electronics Tips

- Look for energy-saving ENERGY STAR home electronics.
- Unplug appliances, or use a power strip and use the switch on the power strip to cut all power to the appliance, to avoid "vampire" loads. Many appliances continue to draw a small amount of power when they are switched off. These vampire loads occur in most appliances that use electricity, such as DVD players, TVs, stereos, computers, and kitchen

appliances. Unplug battery chargers when the batteries are fully charged or the chargers are not in use.
- Use rechargeable batteries for products like cordless phones and digital cameras. Studies have shown they are more cost effective than disposable batteries. If you must use disposables, check with your trash removal company about safe disposal options.

Use Smart Power Strips to Save Energy
Many electronics go into standby mode when you turn them off. Reduce wasted (vampire) power by plugging electronics into a smart power strip, which can turn your electronics off completely.

Renewable Energy

You have many options for using renewable energy at home including solar panels and small wind turbines.

Solar panels are the most popular form of renewable energy today. You can use them to generate heat, electricity, and indoor and outdoor light.

If you live on at least one acre of land with an ample wind resource, you can generate your own electricity using a small wind electric system. You can also use a small wind turbine for pumping water, or to charge a sailboat battery.

You may have also heard of using a geothermal or ground-source heat pump to heat and cool your home. While not technically a renewable energy technology, this energy-saving technology makes use of the constant temperature near the earth's surface for heating and cooling. See the Heating and Cooling section for more information.

In addition to using renewable energy in your home, you can buy electricity made from renewable energy like the sun, wind, water, plants, and geothermal from your utility company. Check with your local utility for more information.

Renewable Energy Tips

- Installing solar-powered outdoor pathway lights is one of the easiest ways to use solar energy at home.
- Building a new home is the best time to design and orient the home to take advantage of the sun's rays. A well-oriented home lets in the winter sun

Use Solar Power to Heat Water and More!
Today's solar power is highly efficient. You can buy systems to heat your water, provide electricity, and even offload your home heating system.

Small Wind Electric Systems

A small wind turbine system can provide additional electricity in your home, or even power your sailboat battery.

Is a Solar Power System Right for Me?

You could consider adding a solar power system to your house if your location has adequate solar resources. A shade-free, south-facing location is best. At least one of the following should also be true:

- You live in a remote location and your home is not connected to the utility grid. Using solar power might cost you less than extending a power line to the grid. Your power provider will connect your solar system to the electricity grid and credit your bill for any excess power you produce.
- You are willing to pay more up front to reduce the environmental impact of your electricity use.
- Your state, city, or utility offers rebates, tax credits, or other incentives. Visit dsireusa.org to find out about financial incentives in your area.

in south-facing windows to reduce heating bills, and blocks the heat from summer sun to reduce cooling bills (see the Solar Heating and Cooling section).

- Heating water is a great use of solar power (see the Water Heating section). If you have a swimming pool or hot tub, you can use solar power to cut pool heating costs. Most solar pool heating systems are cost competitive with conventional systems and have very low operating costs. It's actually the most cost-effective use of solar energy.
- Installing small wind turbines, which range in size from 400 W to 20 kW, can provide some of the electricity for your home. Other uses of micro wind turbines (20-500 W) include charging batteries for sailboats and other recreational vehicles. Learn more at energysavers.gov.

$ Long-Term Savings Tip

If you've already made your home as energy efficient as possible, and you still have high electricity bills and have access to a good solar resource, you might want to consider generating your own electricity with a solar power system. Solar panels can be easily installed onto ground- or roof-mounted racks, and new products are available that integrate solar cells with the roof, making them much less visible than older systems.

You should consider several factors if you want to install a solar power system, such as your solar resources, siting and sizing the system, the type of system (grid-connected or stand-alone), and electrical safety. Because of the complexity and need for proper installation, it's best to have a professional solar contractor install your system.

Transportation

In 2010, Americans traveled a total of 3 trillion miles—the equivalent of 6.5 million round-trips to the moon.[5]

Transportation accounts for 72% of U.S. oil use, mostly for gas.[6] Luckily, there are plenty of ways to improve your gas mileage or avoid using gas altogether.

Driving Tips*

- Avoid idling. Think about it—idling gets you 0 miles per gallon. The best way to warm up a vehicle is to drive it. No more than 30 seconds of idling on winter days is needed. Anything more simply wastes fuel and increases emissions.
- Avoid aggressive driving, such as speeding, rapid acceleration, and hard braking, which can lower your highway gas mileage by up to 33% and your city mileage by 5%.
- Avoid high speeds. Above 60 mph, gas mileage drops rapidly. For every 5 mph above 60 mph, it's like paying an additional $0.30 per gallon of gasoline.
- Avoid keeping heavy items in your car; an extra 100 pounds in your vehicle could increase your gas costs by up to $.08 cents per gallon.
- Reduce drag by placing items inside the car or trunk rather than on roof racks, which can decrease your fuel economy by 5% or more.
- Combine errands. Several short trips, each one taken from a cold start, can use twice as much fuel as one trip covering the same distance when the engine is warm.

Car Maintenance Checklist

✓ Use the right grade of motor oil for your car

✓ Keep tires properly inflated and aligned

✓ Get regular tune ups and maintenance checks

✓ Replace clogged air filters

check out:
www.fueleconomy.gov

- Check into telecommuting, carpooling, and public transit to save driving and car maintenance costs. Many urban areas provide carpool lanes that are usually less congested, which means you will get to work and home faster and more refreshed!

Car Maintenance Tips

- Use the grade of motor oil your car's manufacturer recommends. Using a different motor oil can lower your gas mileage by 1%-2%.
- Inflate your tires to the pressure listed in your owner's manual or on a sticker in the glove box or driver's side door jamb. This number may differ from the maximum pressure listed on your tire's sidewall.

* All cost estimates assume an average price of $3.96 per gallon. *Source: fueleconomy.gov*

- Get regular maintenance checks to avoid fuel economy problems due to worn spark plugs, dragging brakes, sagging belts, low transmission fluid, or transmission problems.
- Don't ignore the check-engine light—it can alert you to problems that affect fuel economy as well as more serious problems, even when your vehicle seems to be running fine.
- Replace clogged air filters on an older car with a carbureted engine to improve gas mileage by as much as 10% and to protect your engine.

$ Long-Term Savings Tips

Choose vehicles according to your need. For example, if you mostly drive in cities, a smaller hybrid might be right for you because they get better mileage in city driving and are easier to park.

If you need a vehicle for towing or heavy use, consider a clean diesel vehicle. Diesel engines are quieter, more powerful, and 30%-35% more efficient than similar-sized gasoline engines. The new generation of clean diesel vehicles must meet the same emissions standards as gasoline vehicles.

Many vehicles produced by U.S. auto manufacturers are flexible fuel vehicles (FFVs), which can run on E85 (85% ethanol, 15% gasoline) and other ethanol-gasoline blends. Check your owner's manual to find out if your vehicle is an FFV.

Consider buying a highly fuel-efficient vehicle. A fuel-efficient, plug-in electric (PHEV), hybrid, or alternative fuel vehicle could cut your fuel costs and help the environment. See the Fuel

Drive an Energy Efficient Vehicle
You can save money and help the environment by driving a highly energy-efficient vehicle. Check out other options such as public transportation and riding your bike to work.

Economy Guide at fueleconomy.gov for more information on buying a new fuel-efficient car or truck.

Also, if you have a plug-in hybrid electric or an all-electric vehicle, charging stations for electric vehicles are increasingly available throughout the country. Similarly, you can find alternative fuel stations—such as those that offer E85—and charging sites by visiting the Alternative Fueling Station Locator online at afdc.energy.gov/afdc/locator/stations.

References

Alternative Fuels and Advanced
Vehicles Data Center
Afdc.energy.gov

American Council for an
Energy-Efficient Economy
Aceee.org/consumer

Cool Roof Rating Council
Coolroofs.org

Database of State Incentives for
Renewables & Efficiency (DSIRE)
Dsireusa.org

DOE Building America
BuildingAmerica.gov

DOE Building Technologies Program
Buildings.energy.gov

DOE Building Technologies Program,
2010 Buildings Energy Databook
Buildingsdatabook.eren.doe.gov

DOE Energy Information Administration
Residential Energy Consumption Survey
Eia.doe.gov/emeu/recs/contents.html

DOE/EPA Fuel Economy Guide
Fueleconomy.gov

DOE Federal Energy Management Program
Eere.energy.gov/femp

DOE Office of Electricity Delivery
and Energy Reliability
Oe.energy.gov

Energy Savers
Energysavers.gov

ENERGY STAR®
Energystar.gov

Green Roofs for Healthy Cities
Greenroofs.org

National Renewable Energy Laboratory
Nrel.gov

Oak Ridge National Laboratory
Ornl.gov

Rocky Mountain Institute Home
Energy Briefs
Rmi.org

Smart Grid
Smartgrid.gov

Energy Assessment Professionals

Nationally-certified energy auditors are
listed with the following organizations:

Building Performance Institute
Bpi.org

National Association of Home Builders
Nahb.com

North American Technician Excellence
Natex.org

Residential Energy Services Network
Resnet.us

Endnotes

1. Lawrence Berkeley National Laboratory, The Potential for Reducing Urban Air Temperatures and Energy Consumption Through Vegetative Cooling, eec.ucdavis.edu/ACEEE/1994-96/1994/VOL04/155.PDF

2. Lawrence Berkeley National Laboratory, The Potential for Reducing Urban Air Temperatures and Energy Consumption Through Vegetative Cooling, eec.ucdavis.edu/ACEEE/1994-96/1994/VOL04/155.PDF

3. Energystar.gov, Water Heater, Whole Home Gas Tankless, energystar.gov/index.cfm?fuseaction=find_a_product showProductGroup&pgw_code=WH

4. 2010 Buildings Energy Data Book, buildings databook.eren.doe.gov

5. U.S. Department of Transportation press release March 2, 2011: Nation's Highway Traffic Reaches Highest Level Since 2007, www.dot.gov/affairs/2011/fhwa0311.html

6. U.S. Energy Information Administration, U.S. Primary Energy Flow by Source and Sector, 2009, eia.gov/totalenergy/data/annual/pecss_diagram.cfm